A GHOSTING IN UKRAINE

A GHOSTING IN UKRAINE

Patricia McCarthy

DARE-GALE PRESS

First published in Great Britain by Dare-Gale Press, 2023

www.daregale.com

ISBN 9781915968012

Thanks to James Harpur for his special inspiration throughout this sequence, and to Paul O'Prey and David Pollard for their close attention to the poems. Also to the editors of the following publications in which a number of these poems first appeared: *The Guardian* ('Four Seasons Gone', Poem of the Week); *The Irish Times* ('Coda', Saturday Poem of the Week); *Temenos* ('Chagall's memory of the Pogroms') and *Poetry and All That Jazz* ('Letter to Tchaikovsky').

Front cover image: 'Children in Church' (detail), by Kateryna Kosianenko. Reproduced by kind permission of the artist.

Font: Typeset in 10/11pt Delicato, designed by Stefan Hattenbach.

Printed in England by One Digital Brighton on GF Smith Munken paper which is certified by both Cradle to Cradle and the Forest Stewardship Council. Dare-Gale Press is committed to environmentally conscious publishing. For our environmental policy please visit www.daregale.com.

A Ghosting in Ukraine

Akhmatova,

is it you weaving in and out of the catalpa trees
a small glass of pepper vodka in your hand,
the satchel full of books from your loathed law studies
dumped, with empty perfume bottles, on the ground?

Is it your girlish outline I see dancing in windows
of concertina-ed years, you hiding behind huge cages
of watermelons on street corners from the shadows
of unshaven sailors, saving your virgin pages

from hulks of ships blacker than the blackest sea,
Rilke, Homer, Dante already inscribed upon your breath?
Akhmatova, gone from here, an infant with your family –
Odesa claimed you, despite your living and dead deaths.

It espied you on local visits with your 'scarred heart',
hiding yourself in alleys of the nobleman's park
with your aquiline nose, snubbing every horse and cart.
Ghost over ghost, you made yourself up, made your mark

in cobbled squares as if mounted on a proud Cossack horse
of your ancestry, in your blood the boast of Genghis Khan...
How they need you now, at your Aunty Vakar's house
in Kyiv or at your mother's grave in Derazhnia Raion

to speak arias rather than folk tunes, and stand at the gate
of their suffering, clutching thin hands through iron bars
as if each was your son's. Fate repeats fate –
while you fade into pond waters under the nenuphars.

Wild Horses of Chernobyl

Where are you, wild horses of Chernobyl?

Did you think it thunder: the rumbling
of Russian tanks in the no man's land

now a nature reserve – as the earth
churned by their heavy tracks put you

at a renewed risk of contamination?
Maybe you sensed the sudden levels

of radiation climbing the trees
sky-high, and warned the wolves, bison,

brown bears, elk and lynx – all birdsong
on hold. Ghosts in a ghost town,

whited out by blizzards, you shelter,
at times with dogs, once pets,

in ground floors of derelict office blocks,
looking out onto woods red-dead

from dust. I imagine you, wild horses,
pushing through walls of deserted kindergartens,

picking up limbs between your teeth
to put back onto cherished, abandoned dolls –

spooking at memories of dizzy horses
on carrousels, plastic peeling off.

But come, wild horses of Chernobyl,
gallop away – through Pripyat, Skavutych

to Kyiv where wide-eyed children, vulnerable
as you, will climb onto your backs

from their mothers' arms for transport
to the Carpathian mountains. There

neither they, nor you, need ever be ghosts
again in that place where you could die

at a touch. With coats still the colour
of the Gobi desert you came from, and manes

stiff as brushes to sweep missiles from skies,
the Spring will be more than a glimpse

of green from crevices in a mildewed hotel
once full of guests. And O, wild horses, may you

breed fillies and colts that whinny
through the valleys of our hearts and minds

for the innocents sacrificed everywhere.

Letter to Tchaikovsky

i

Borders crossed through you,
Belarus, Russia, Ukraine,
kept changing in your veins.
Music, though, was your mainland.

As a small child, your fingers knew
notes by tapping on a windowpane,
your inborn gift for original refrains
a future already in your piano hands

until the glass shattered into bits
of ice, jewel-lit by the sun. Piodr.
As you grew into theory: harmony,

instrumentation, counterpoint
and composition, you aimed forever
to keep that shattering in a melody

ii

Russia claimed you though it tried
to hide your attraction to bearded men,
focusing on the women who fell for you.
Most at home in Ukraine, you stayed

on your sister's estate, a place to hide
amongst a blue river, waterfalls, glens,
your feet marking time in feverfew,
lemon balm, chamomile while you played

concertos and symphonies in your head.
And another border – between Russia
and Europe – tried to fight over

your influences as you hummed ballads
sung by blind musicians and gardeners,
skipping rhymes in the reddest clover –

iii
never quite one thing, it seemed, or another...
In composing piano pieces, you recalled,
always, the duets performed with your sister,
Swan Lake, inspired by your nieces, nephews –

ballets, *The Sleeping Beauty, Nutcracker,*
to great applause. Your inspiration never stalled.
After a breakup with your patron, Nadezhda –
the blackness in chords you outgrew.

And now the villa where you stayed in Trostianets:
reduced to rubble, the doors of your museum
broken, walls damaged, even your statue,

still upright, riddled with bullet holes. Yet
an overture, behind the shells' pandemonium,
is turning the shattering into a melody.

Letter to Chagall

You nearly lost your home, built, brick
by brick, by your father, a shop of victuals
slanted to the side. And in they trooped, oils

still wet: the Hassidic Jews like you –
from your canvases on which, instead
of black and white, they were delineated

in blue, yellow and green, transcending
old bigotries. The cobbler and fiddler
you saved from pogroms by flying them over

roofs and towers, enrolling them in circuses
whose big tops ballooned with mountain air
purged of nationality and creed. And Bella,

your beautiful Bella, who waited so long
to marry you, stayed quietly in the town
while guns blasted, bombs rained down –

when your house held its quickened breath,
miraculously escaping ruin. You knew
what it felt: to tread rubble, joists askew –

to pick up shards of memory, the necks
of glass bottles, samovars shone by your mother,
a cracked snuff box from your uncle's cellar.

To prevent produce dropping from baskets,
your father had rounded the house's corners –
and life-long you preserved those corners

floating brush-stroked bridal couples
amongst stars, while equestriennes with wings
piaffed through space: nothing sharp cutting

calligraphy from the Torah scrolls. Chagall –
you constructed, unlike your father-builder,
walls of paint behind which you stayed forever,

despite the claim on you of Paris. And still
you invite Akhmatova, Gogol, Shevchenko,
Prokofiev, Tchaikovsky, blacksmiths

bakers, chimney sweeps into the hallway
of your home, orange doors thrown open, the arts
and trades all one, its foundations dug into your heart.

Chagall's memory of the Pogroms

You remembered them as a child
from your house in Pokrovskaya Street:
the distant cries, then the shooting
of Jews herded into the market square
while a string quartet tried to play,
the faces of perpetrators recognised
as acquaintances by those who survived.
You remembered the strange feel
of walking as if through coiled wire
through violently-shaved beards
that littered the ground, the way hairs,
suddenly silky, stuck to your soles.
Black marks of a black time.
And you saw them: these scenes
reflected in the Western Dvina waters,
their surreal glints in the midday sun
like crafted shards of stained glass
from some bulging Orthodox church,
its ceiling the animated sky
invented by angels and lovers.
You kept the torn photograph of a woman
holding a baby that, years later,
fully-grown, raped her; a shoemaker
killed by a neighbour whose worn boots
he had only recently repaired.
You never painted these
nor the long black frockcoats of your kind
hanging like vampires' wings upside down
from silver birches. You knew your father
was vulnerable as he worked in the ghetto,
lifting heavy barrels of herrings,
stirring tiny slippery fish with frozen hands.
Maybe it was the light on his overalls
from herring brine that you were always
trying to capture between your frames.
And when you couldn't sleep, I imagine
you pretended the world you saw
was a nightmare that a lullaby could cure.

Hanging out washing in Kyiv

Bend and stretch, stretch and bend:
the women hang out their laundry
across verandahs, streets, gardens.

bed-linen frayed by intimacies,
civvies discarded by their men
drafted to war zones in a time warp,

it seems – now is then, then now,
here is there, and there here –
bend and stretch, stretch and bend...

the notches on their thin spines
like beads offered up to make amends
for the stains in hearts too indelible

for detergents, the washing lines
latitudes dividing two worlds.
And the women wait, biting nails,

willing a wind to flesh out garments,
their men rescued from death tolls.
Fold and flatten, fold and flatten –

their untutored ballet too desperate
for any choreographer – as hopes drain
from wicker baskets, and pegs let

the last remnants of the recent drop,
like telegraphs of old, into apron pockets.
Bend and stretch, stretch and bend...

And the women wait for a feather to float –
under a sky that rumbles no godsend –
a plume pen from a crane, storm-petrel,

white stork. Their letters fly up, up,
into the space where body meets soul...
and we are but pinpricks in the ether.

Bend and stretch, stretch and bend...
remember the lines of Akhmatova,
Mandelstam, their feather nibs of Dante.

Two letters to Mandelstam

i

'We live, but feel no land at our feet.'

Dear Osip,
Through shadows I see you strolling
along a cobbled street, tuning yourself
like an instrument, your moving lips

composing in time to your every step...
slow, stately, quick – your march changes
tempo to your every thought, no need

for paper that might incriminate you.
As if on a cellphone, you are the madman
that you became, your odd ventriloquy

without sound. Nadezhda, your bride
from Kyiv, follows life-long the fate-line
in your hand that takes you, expelled,

on transport trains into the 'open loins
of the Steppes', compounds of transit camps...
Voronezh, Tashkent, Vladivostok. All the time

you learn by heart your poems, each one
a house in which to live, protected, yourself
the architect of clean lines, plain décor,

on the roof-tiles white storks nesting for luck.
And your special spade, always with you,
digging into the garden of your psyche.

It seems, outdoing archeologists, you find
at last, under your feet, land beyond the gulags,
and that elusive nugget – harmony.

ii

Dear Osip,
How lucky you were to meet Nadezhda
in a nightclub in Kyiv and then to evolve:
her eyes your own, even your words hers.

Perfect she was as your scribe, editor,
recording drafts of poems, keeping the secret
of coded lines. When you finally agreed

that manuscripts were more lasting than you,
she handwrote what you dictated
in exercise book after exercise book –

then tore out the pages as if tearing off wings
to scatter like loaves and fishes
amongst friends she could trust – a jigsaw

of sequences safeguarded from suppression.
She it was who helped you push off
your shoulder the dumb, doom-filled raven,

and invited goldfinches in to the cottage
in Stary Krym, your retreat from work trips
to St Petersburg, Leningrad, Moscow.

You could hear Armenian monks chanting
from the Surp Khack monastery when the wind
blew towards you from the Grytsia mountain

and you both joined in. You told him to ignore
black bonnets of sunflowers born in mourning,
heads hung, the ears of corn deafened

by revolution and war. And to remember instead
younger days in Odesa when you danced together
under the arches of magnolias, drank

cucumber toilet-water. How her *Memoirs*
float, Osip, in the paper houseboats of your poems
that you captain along the horizon towards hope.

'This land is in blood'

'This land is in blood: A Ukraine village digs up the dead.'
Economic Times, India, April 17, 2022

I

Casket-maker

No identity, yet there he is: a local smallholder
the secret saviour – like a composer as he whispers
and kisses wrought-iron crosses on familiar graves.
.

Installation artists could learn from him when he bends
and rips cardboard, stitching up corrugated sections
with reeds from banks of a pond now an empty crater.

Aesthetic as any designer, he tears lace from the hems
of petticoats worn by generations of grandmothers
in Mykulychi, their ghost footsteps tap-tapping

in time to the taps of walnuts that fall from the trees
lining at intervals the quiet street. How carefully he edges
with the white lace strips the makeshift caskets measured

with his eye – to give dignity to the fresh corpses shot
on doorsteps, four on the same day. Then the lifting
and laying of them, hands bound with rosaries, eyes

charcoal-rimmed. And the digging with a dented shovel,
sweat beads threading themselves onto the rosary beads.
The earth, innocent until lately as himself, he scoops

with a bent back and flings into the hole as if he has planted
wheat or rapeseed balked by the war, these days, of its season.
No objections to be made of the picnic tables that appear

customarily for the bereaved to pay their shocked respects
while trying to adjust to new wastelands. Unifier of the arts,
words his gestures, he sniffs the coming lilac blooms.

II

A Rallying Cry

Come on, poets of insides and outsides,
of regular and irregular far-flung places –

would you have torn up your books:
published and unpublished, sequences,

pamphlets, collected and selected, signed,
numbered – and soaked them in the pain

of a distant nation to make *papier-maché* coffins,
sonnets, odes, ghazals, experimental verses

mixed with the blood and bone-meal leaking
from corpses, too strong for fecund growth,

too burning, for any plant? How many of you
would forsake your egos – forget the need

for your name in posterity, your emotions petty,
so petty and beyond elegies beside the ultimate zero?

How many of you would embrace a creed,
any creed, to carry you through, and still believe

in a life left to be lived, your handwriting, practised
scarcely now, suddenly everyone's, its italics

and loops not your own? Come on, poets – how many
of you would donate your own blood and bone

to be sprinkled, just sprinkled to give flowers, fruits,
onions, garlic and parsnip for where gardens

have vanished? Simply remember how tiny feet
of birds still print far-flung lines on wastes of sand.

III

A Kind of Triptych

i

Ira Slepchenko, new widow,
stands motionless, face impassive,
in denial. She cannot believe
Sasha Nedolezhko, her husband

could be this shape, as at a stage show –
so recently breathing, active –
in a blanket, then body-bag to receive
a war crime inspection at the demand

of some official. Like a marble angel,
attached to a fancy tomb, she, too,
is surreal, the smoke from her cigarette

set in a solid line, her tears, unable
to flow, are stones that cannot undo
the clasp of unending death on the casket.

ii

Valya Naumenko embraces Ira
as if, no artist, she is painting them
onto a canvas she neither bought
nor sold in any marketplace she knows.

This resembles the rule of the Fűhrer
studied at school, history's theorems
on Russia never proved or disproved. Caught
off-guard here, she and Ira clean windows,

scrub floors, as neighbours, face to face
over daily gossip and chores; none of this
swirling ether that surrounds them now

while the canvas stretches slowly into space
upon space – no sky, nothing to miss
but brushstrokes forwards, back on a plough.

iii

Irina Voronete is hiding away in her house
next to the cemetery. She has seen the sky
turn to concrete and crash into the earth,
the stars'eyes put out by missiles; her hair

has become a grey cloud overnight. Without gas,
electricity, water, she rocks to the melody
of her home-grown potatoes boiling in the dearth.
The news is depressing in the wood-warmed air:

her small radio stays turned off. She composes
her own ditties and tunes as she cuts radishes.
She cannot rival medieval chants, Akhmatova,

Mandelstam. She no longer supposes
a stork has landed for luck on her roof; wishes
its red beak did not look dipped in terror.

iv

When the young Russian soldiers come,
Irina offers them milk from her only cow.
They take her cell phone but that is all.

They weep at such a kind welcome,
then sigh that they do not want war now.
Ira, Valya, Irina hold hands under their shawls.

Postscript to Ahkmatova

Golden-lipped Anna...

In the *balakhan* you shared, Nadezhda watched
the voice in your lips, the lips in your voice
as you summoned from your childhood

the hippodrome where piebald ponies circled.
Behind your lips Nazedha heard organ-grinders,
knife-grinders, tinsmiths, rag-and-bone dealers

in need of you to scrape evil off back yards.
When you pressed your lips tighter together,
Nadezhda felt you interpreting for the wounded

the trees' shade, the gush of water that relieved
the noonday heat. She saw you spit out,
without spitting, the rank scars of trenches

in the rose-breath of the Summer Garden,
drum-rolls in the deep-frozen Field of Mars,
black gangs of crows caw-cawing still

over the lines of those led out for execution.
In the *balakhan* you shared, Nadezhda looked
at your lips butterfly-brushing your voice's range.

Bring them back...

Bring them back:
Mussorgsky, Borodin, Prokofiev –
the composers, pianists, conductors.
Let Rachmaninov's giant hands
stretch to twelve notes
instead of an octave to span
his native land overshadowed
by Russia on ivories innocent of war.
Let virtuoso new pieces
which only he can play
take his name through trashed towns
and territories of cows and goats.
See girls in their prom dresses
stand stock still on the rubble
of ballrooms, feet stripped of rhythms.
Make them proud again to belong
to Ukraine; return the folksongs
from fields and mix them with echoes
of Kyivan chant and bells
from gilded domes rather than elegies
of the Neva. Dare them to use
the curse words introduced by Gogol
instead of guns – and invent
stories for their children
to induce beauty sleeps. Let birds
announce new names for spaces
once filled with houses and streets,
fighter jets turn into paper planes
returning the dead to be endeared.
Bring them all back,
with their lost birthplaces
and inner steppes. Their bars
of music overlap borders,
belong to every land and time.

Children in the Church

After a painting by Kateryna Kosianenko

The children huddle in what remains
of the church, its roof peepholed by stars.
Like tiny squabs fallen from nests, they
try out their voices, half-talk, half-song:

Kyivan chants learnt like skipping rhymes
by heart: the *Kyrie, In the Dark Night, Credo,*
no angel wings lent to their monodies –
simply the massive spread of feathers

of the Paraclete accustomed to pervading
all lives. Parents and siblings seem
to have vanished through trap doors
where jugglers of souls fall over

their own feet and disbelievers drop
into the lines of Dante. You want to steal
for them the Byzantine gold from backgrounds
of the icons that insist on appearing

as if for class acts from the remaining wall
behind the desecrated altar; to extract haloes
for use as hoola hoops around wrist-sized waists.
You can see dark is more familiar to them

than daylight, and watch them kick bricks
like punctured footballs as they balance on rubble.
Turn them round and around till they play catch
with ringmasters and clowns, the past present,

the present past. And wait for the wall
as it sways to reveal their faces fresh as blooms
once adorning naves. The children huddle
in what remains of the church. Only memories
mend loved ones until they, too, are gone.

The Future Conditional

The only bullets here: mast acorns
that cannot fire, brought down by gales.

They skid through them: the refugees
on their way to a language lesson

in the village hall. The teacher opens
her kind, painted heart, reputations

for canes and dunces' corners
obliterated in the dust from the chalk

supplied for the blackboard. Hanging
on to their past existences like lifelines,

they are not sure they want to learn what
she imparts: tongue-twisters, fricatives

between her lips of unfamiliar plosives,
conjugations: the present perfect,

future conditional, the past past.
Reluctant to wear Englishness inside

and out, they need only phrases to get by.
And secretly preserve in burnt-out diaries

and prayer-books their own language.
On the return to host families, they see

their reflections congregate in shop windows
as if back in named home streets. The trees

haven't yet lost their heads – and they keep
theirs under a risen Hunter's moon, waiting

to inherit an oral lesson from morning birds
that sing, through wreathed mists, in tongues.

Return of the Night-Witches

For the female aviators from the Soviet Union who fought in
World War Two against the Nazis, nick-named 'night-witches'.

Listen out for a certain whooshing
when, on both or no sides at once,
they intercept missiles and drones.

In plywood frames, canvas-covered,
their planes, light and slow, land
everywhere and nowhere. We won't see

the fresh-faced girl pilots, lips
painted with navigational pencils
behind besoms of control-sticks, boots

size 42, too big for most of them,
uniforms tailored for chunkier men.
In exposed cock-pits, we might glimpse

a wisp of hair newly-cut and think it
a boy's torn by whipping winds – or
the curve grey-yellow of a cheek waxed

by frostbite. As they swoop low to pick
stork feathers off roofs, sunflowers
not yet in mourning, they might drop –

onto raised ground-levels of rubble,
for the tears, wrung hands and cries
of terrified children – doves' wings

collected from the Holy Ghost, rays
of grace from a supernatural sun.
Hard to target, with a slow stall-speed,

they are here for us in squadrons, killing
their engines when any enemy looms,
poised for attack, yet chorusing

Pax, Pax Vobiscum. We won't notice
the extra pulse from Akhmatova's poems,
and the notes from Shostakovich

crashing into crescendos from Tashkent
to sustain them in the scarred skies
they upturn to take on space. Remember,

they have learned lessons from that old war,
which should never be repeated. And
they wait for us to join them as they loop

the loop through their own mandalas,
trailing the flowers they drew by hand
on fuselages in a tailback of stars.

Coda

Sing, Tyra, Svetlana, Viktoria,
what you sang on baptisms, birthdays,
weddings – requiems now echoing
only behind your eyes. Let local feet

tap you into the *Fleadh* – as harmonica,
fiddle, tin-whistle carry you away
to town squares back home. Sing
and dance on, celebrating the meet

of countries as flags flap and you are
safe with what you never imagined:
Akhmatova, disguised as a Saint,

here in the tesserae in Mullingar.
Stories behind stories like yours behind
the pose, her gracious restraint.

*

You might have heard of him in Kharkiv
where he studied Law: the man she called
the love of her life before his chosen exile,

his serial philandering hard to forgive:
the man with the massive, sensuous build
who created her here in the side-chapel

like a jigsaw in bits of glass, marble, gold,
his cutting-hammer, gum, horn-handled knife,
the flick of his wrist as he specialised,
after a forty-year absence, in her head, hands,

restoring a youth unable to grow old –
and perhaps the secret preserved beyond life
of a matched passion she never surmised
from him, Boris Anrep, in time's quicksands.

*

Sing, Tyra, Svetlana, Viktoria –
as Akhmatova did to the one preserved
in her heart. Those you have lost
will stay as dreams and live on.
Dance to heard and unheard melodeons.

Night on Bald Mountain, near Kyiv

For Carol Rumens and i.m. Yuri Drobyshev

i

Akhmatova, you must be hovering
on your birthday, St John's eve,

around the forbidden Bald Mountain
Lysa Hora, shaved by witches who visit
from covens, cemeteries, ruins.

It might be you winding the front line
around what resembles the scalp

of a despot no one claims – tighter
and tighter until it breaks. And down
rush ghosts of the young soldiers

lost on both sides, bloodless hands
reaching out to grasp one another

in friendship, hatchets buried in mists.
As severed lifelines dangle from besoms
and brooms, you would be torn apart,

Akhmatova, with your love for Russia
and Ukraine, and would surely join in,

hanging on to the cats' and dogs' tails
of the witches you make white who push
the devil over a precipice – sliding with you

like athletes from the rounded slopes
into a Sabbath never before known.

ii

You might be listening hard
to Mussorgsky's tone-poem, 'Night
on Bald Mountain', hear witches,

not quite angels, coming and going,
ransacking his staves, collecting,
for your 'Requiem', cuttings of spurge,

lungwort, berry yew, Cossack Juniper –
from stubble tangled with bracken,
gorse and thorn trees. You might think

even the mountain an invention
then, now, for non-existent treaties –
as threnodies, composed by winds, resound

from crooked Zherep pine forests
on their way up to you. You might catch
broken-down warhorses stamping far off,

extract stories of stories, stories within
stories from each blood-donated note,
inventing prophetic longer life-histories

for the boy ghosts taken before their time.
Your voice has its own narrative,
its own orchestra. Your body of poetry,

often banned, cannot die, the rhythms
of its ghosts come and go, every lost boy
you decorate with sakura, evergreen barberry.

Ammo Boxes from Ukraine

For Oleksandr Klymenko and Sofia Atlantova, artists from
Kyiv – sales from their painted ammo boxes go towards the
Pirogov First Volunteer mobile hospital in the Donbas region.

Our Lady of the Seven Arrows
Our Lady of the Never Fading Blossom
Our Lady of the Crop Saver...

Silent witnesses of war – how easily
the ammunitions boxes open, like Pandora's,
to release all traces of conflict: the stench

of ignited gunpowder, wings made from
punctured lungs of the dead, pewter-gray,
frostbitten extremities. How swifty

they metamorphose off the front line
into collectors' items, gold from Byzantium
on their brush-stroked surfaces; saints

on the rough plywood reminiscent
of traditional blessed boards, interiors
tabernacles for old and new Hosts flanked

by attar-scented angels with kingfishers' wings.
Edged by clasps, locks, latches, they could be
reliquaries for popular tunes, jewelry. Yet watch

thuribles swing as the painted icons glow
for lives sacrificed. And the boxes' silence prays
for terrain without land to become land again.

Saint George and the Dragon
Saint Nicholas with a long beard
Archangel Michael on a white horse

Nina

Your name echoed through our childhood.
We made up ball-bouncing rhymes with it,
pictured you as a plastic bride on a cake,

teased my father about you, his sweetheart
before his love at first sight for my mother.
We never stopped to query what you

were doing in Hong Kong: a White Russian
from the Shliakhta class in Ukraine.
We simply pictured you on my father's ship,

HMS *Tamar*, sipping cocktails, a frieze
of sampans and junks behind you. I wonder
if he told you how he spoke with the winds

and taught them to recite the Hail Mary;
if he read the stars to you, introduced you
to the spirit of each wave and dredged up

shanties from the coral-lit fathoms already
in his heart. Maybe he confessed he was married
to the sea as, onshore, he drove you to the Peak,

wove stories around the ancient Banyan tree,
put an arm through yours in Repulse Bay.
Nina, our bouncing-ball-rhyme Nina – I see you:

high cheekbones, glamorous – such a shame
we never got to know you in person when,
in your eighth and ninth decades, you lived only

two Kentish roads from our widowed mother.
We would have inquired about the slither
of the Pearl River beside which you settled

with nightmares about the Bolsheviks you escaped.
You could have told us more about the Irish charm
of our father, retrieving from his ghost the ladies' man.

Four Seasons Gone

For the outpouring of poems by many who have never written
poems before in Ukraine during the war.

There can be no canticles, matins, evensong,
no waiting for blue irises, cherries to come along
in their own season, with four seasons gone.

How bravely you bear witness, testify tight-lipped,
with scribbles on wings, inscribing verses
on the green scum of ponds, passing hearses
pattering your lines. And your words creep

into the cracks in syllables fractured by shells;
then steal from town squares swung tongues of bells.

Following the Stations of each patriot's Cross,
you throw lifelines across pages to forestall loss.

The light, with no warning, has been burgled by dark.
There is no war, the Kremlin insists, trench-talk
gagged, missile smoke dismissed as lengths,

for cradles, of organic cotton, bombs
just the claps of an audience at a show. Yet –
over spat-out cherry stones, your poems will go on
daring the unsayable, with four seasons gone.